Alcohol = BUSTED!

Rich Mintzer

Enslow Publishers, Inc.

40 Industrial Road   PO Box 38
Box 398   Aldershot
Berkeley Heights, NJ 07922   Hants GU12 6BP
USA   UK

http://www.enslow.com

Library of Congress Cataloging-in-Publication Data

Mintzer, Richard.
    Alcohol=Busted! / Rich Mintzer.— 1st ed.
      p. cm. — (Busted!)
    Includes bibliographical references and index.
    ISBN 0-7660-2552-7
    1. Alcoholism—Juvenile literature. 2. Alcoholism—United States—Juvenile literature. 3. Teenagers—Alcohol use—Juvenile literature. I. Title. II. Series.
    HV5066.M56 2005
    613.81—dc22

                                             2004019265

Printed in the United States of America

10 9 8 7 6 5 4 3 2 1

To Our Readers: We have done our best to make sure all Internet Addresses in this book were active and appropriate when we went to press. However, the author and the publisher have no control over and assume no liability for the material available on those Internet sites or on other Web sites they may link to. Any comments or suggestions can be sent by e-mail to comments@enslow.com or to the address on the back cover.

Illustration Credits: Courtesy of Lindsey Bauman/ Kansas State Collegian, pp. 4–5, 56–57; Courtesy of California Office of Traffic Safety, pp. 33, 71; Courtesy of CDC–PHIL, p. 51; Corel Corporation, pp. 22, 40, 45, 48; Digital Stock, pp. 7, 77; Courtesy of *Driven Magazine*, a MADD Publication, pp. 59, 68; Courtesy of Carol Friedfel, pp. 10, 17, 42; © 2004 JupiterImages, pp. 14, 35, 46 (background), 74; Courtesy of NHSDA, pp. 53, 65, 66; Courtesy of Jessica Paris, Youth in Action Coordinator, Juno, Alaska chapter, pp. 82, 84.

Cover Illustration: Associated Press.

CONTENTS

1. Getting Caught 5

2. Alcohol Testing 12

3. The History of Alcohol
   in America 20

4. The Effects of Alcohol
   on the Body 39

5. Alcohol and Your
   Social Life 57

6. Needing and Getting
   Help 73

   Glossary 87

   Chapter Notes 91

   Further Reading 100

   Internet Addresses 101

   Index 102

CHAPTER ONE

GETTING CAUGHT

The radio call came in to the police station at around 9:00 P.M. It was a woman complaining about a loud party that was going on in the home next door. "It's been going on for a while and it looks like some kids are hanging out on the front lawn drinking," the woman told the police.[1]

Captain John Kapica has fielded many similar calls in his thirty-three years on the force in the small town of Westchester, New York. He no longer goes to the scene himself, but instead his officers respond to the call.

At 9:30 P.M., six police officers show up outside the house. The officers pull up in unmarked cars so they do not draw attention to themselves. From outside, with their binoculars, they can see what is taking place in the house. Sure enough, kids are drinking beer. They carefully take note of which kids are holding or drinking alcohol. They then look around the yard and see other kids. Some are drinking and others are smoking marijuana.

At 9:40 P.M., two officers move quickly around the back of the house to guard the back door, while two other officers wait on the sides of the house. It looks from the outside as if there may be as many as fifty people in there, mostly teenagers. The remaining two officers come to the front door and knock loudly to be heard over the music. Two adults answer the door. They seem surprised to see the officers.

Once inside the house, the officers order everyone to stop what he or she is doing. The music is

The police officers moved fast to break up the party.

shut off and suddenly everyone freezes. A few kids try to escape through the back door and through an open window, but the cops outside are ready for them. They block the exits, and only a couple of kids get away, while the others have no choice but to remain in the house.

The police tell everyone to sit down. Some argue and complain that they were not doing anything wrong. Others just sit quietly. The officers outside come in, ushering in a few kids who were drinking on the front lawn.

As the officers start getting the names, addresses, and phone numbers of the kids, one officer talks to the two adults. It turns out that they are the parents of one boy who was throwing the party for a friend of his. They say there were only supposed to be fifteen kids at the party, mostly friends of their son from the wrestling team.[2]

"Didn't you notice that there were three times as many kids in your house? Didn't you see all the cars parked outside or hear all of the noise?" asks one of the officers.[3] The parents say that they were in another part of the house. They did not want to interfere with the party. They did not notice that many of the kids at the party were drinking beer and whiskey or taking illegal drugs or doing both.

Now the parents of each kid will have to come and pick him or her up. While they sit waiting, the officers write out a summons for each of the kids they saw drinking or holding alcohol. One officer starts taking photos of the scene—empty beer cans, empty liquor bottles, and bags of marijuana found in the house and in the yard.[4] This will be used as evidence.

Not only are the kids worried about their future, but also the parents whose home this party was in are worried because they too can be charged with contributing to the delinquency of a minor by allowing underage drinking in their home.[5] This charge means that they, as adults, can be held responsible for minors taking part in illegal activities.[6]

Police in the same area of New York State were called to the scene of a different party. This time it was taking place at a hotel. When the officers arrived, the hotel manager met them and led them to a room where the party had been taking place. Apparently the party had been going on for some time and had become rowdy. The officers expected to find adults who had too much to drink and needed to calm down. Instead they found a packed room of teenagers. They arrested twenty-six teenagers, who were charged with possession of alcohol by minors. Two other people were charged with child endangerment, after admitting that they had purchased the alcohol.[7]

Why are these New York cops so busy cracking down on underage drinking? They are trying to stop disasters before they happen. "We don't

Captain John Kapica and other police officers do their best to stop underage drinking.

like busting up parties," says Captain Kapica. "But we have to stop these kids before they get sick, injured, or even killed."[8]

These officers know the story of the thirteen-year-old girl who was assaulted by a drunk sixteen-year-old boy, and the story of the local seventeen-year-old football star at a nearby high school who died after an afternoon beer party in a private home. They also know the story of local high school student Emily B., age seventeen, who died in a car accident. The driver, also a teenager, admitted in court that she and Emily were at the house of a third girl. They had all been drinking alcohol. Emily was just one of several teens in the area to die in car crashes after a night of drinking at local parties.[9]

For these reasons, officers like Dave E. and Captain Kapica now take the job of stopping underage drinking parties very seriously. After Emily's death, the town of Ramapo, New York, created a task force of parents, students, police, school officials, and substance-abuse experts to work together as a team to help prevent more tragedies.

The toughest part of the job for the officers is not breaking up parties but getting the kids to understand that they do not need to drink alcohol to have fun or be cool. As the parents arrive at the scene of the bust, the police release the kids into their parents' custody. Each kid now holds a summons that orders him or her to appear in court. They will have to pay a fine, do several hours of community service, and possibly see an alcohol counselor. Events such as these illustrate clearly to the kids, and their parents, the dangers of underage drinking and the serious consequences that can result from such activities.[10]

CHAPTER TWO

ALCOHOL TESTING

As local police officers tried to wave the student's car over at the checkpoint on Route 26, just outside Purdue University in Indiana, the driver, Michael,* suddenly sped up and took off down the highway. Several of the officers ran to their patrol cars, jumped in, and took off after the driver.

*not his real name

The officers caught up to the vehicle and tried to get Michael to pull over, but he had other plans. He left the campus road and took off onto nearby Jackson Highway, speeding up to eighty miles per hour. The cops were in full pursuit. For the next several minutes, the high-speed chase continued. Then, Michael lost control of the car and veered off the road into a field near an intersection. Michael jumped from the car and ran into the nearby town.

The police officers pulled up alongside of the car. A female passenger was still inside. She told police that she had repeatedly asked Michael to stop and let her go, but he had refused, putting her life in danger.[1]

To find the driver who had run from the car, the local town police called upon the K9 unit. The K9 unit is made up of dogs specifically trained to track down a specific scent. The officers used an article of clothing Michael had left in the car for the dogs to sniff so that they would recognize his scent. With the dogs leading the way, they followed a path from where the car stopped that led into town. After a long search, the dogs helped the officers track Michael down. He was hiding in the yard of a private home. He was

Driving while intoxicated and running from the police will lead to an arrest.

immediately arrested and charged with resisting law enforcement, which refers to avoiding the police, and criminal confinement because he would not let the passenger get out of the car. He was also charged with criminal recklessness with a vehicle (for driving in a dangerous manner), consumption of alcohol by a minor, operating a vehicle under the age of twenty-one with a blood alcohol content of 0.02 percent or higher, and other traffic violations.[2]

The Purdue University Police, working with the local police force, had set up what is called a sobriety checkpoint along one of the roads that leads to and from the college. This was a stopping point on the road where police officers were checking to see if drivers appeared to be sober or drunk. The officers set up such a checkpoint on occasion to help prevent students, or anyone else, from drinking and driving. Each car was stopped at the checkpoint, and the police officers observed the driver, asking him or her a couple of questions, and waved them on. Occasionally an officer would see someone who looked, sounded, or smelled like he or she might have been drinking. The person would be asked to step out of the car. He or she would be given routine sobriety tests like walking a straight line, repeating a sentence, or counting to ten. A field test might also be administered. A field test is where the driver blows into a small tube that indicates whether or not there is alcohol in his or her system.

The driver who had led the officers on a high-speed car chase apparently knew he was driving while under the influence of alcohol, so he drove through the checkpoint without stopping. The police officers at the checkpoint immediately sprang into action by getting into their police cars. They wanted to stop the driver before he caused an accident.[3]

Testing for Alcohol

Alcohol testing is very important for law enforcement officers because the results can show the effects of alcohol on the body. The tests will tell the officers how much alcohol is in the person's bloodstream. The higher the level of alcohol found, the more effect it has on the mind and body.

Each state has laws that limits how much alcohol can be in a person's body when he or she drives a car, or when he or she is considered to be intoxicated. Typically, if the alcohol level in the body is 0.08 percent or higher, it is against the law to drive a car in any state. While this seems like a very low number (less than 1 percent) it can affect the way a person reacts and makes quick decisions.

According to Mothers Against Drunk Driving (MADD), a 170-pound man would have to

A breath alcohol detector, like this one, can detect the presence of alcohol by measuring the amount of alcohol in the blood by testing exhaled air.

consume four drinks in an hour to reach a level of 0.08 percent alcohol in his blood system and a 137-pound woman would need three drinks.[4]

Test results will indicate the severity of the offense. Anyone caught driving a car with a blood alcohol level over the amount allowed by law will receive a driving while intoxicated (DWI) charge or a driving under the influence (DUI) charge. Some states use DWI, while others use DUI. There is no real difference other than the wording.

Either charge will go on the driver's record and can result in paying fines or having a license suspended. Having a suspended license means that a person loses his or her driver's license for an extended period of time. Driving while one's license is suspended is a serious crime. If an underage driver is tested and any alcohol shows up at all, he or she can be fined, ordered to do hours of community service, and have his or her license suspended.

Alcohol Testing Devices

The alcohol saliva test, created in 1988, is a simple and fast test that uses saliva on a special test pad. The test pad changes color in two minutes, and depending on the color, it can tell how much alcohol is in the saliva. The test can also detect if there is alcohol in another substance such as a glass of water or soda.

The breath alcohol detector, also called a Breathalyzer™, is used by the police in many states. The breath alcohol test measures the amount of alcohol in the blood by testing exhaled air. The test is performed by blowing into a breath machine fifteen minutes after alcohol consumption. The test determines how much alcohol it takes to raise the blood alcohol level to a dangerous level.[5]

CHAPTER THREE

THE HISTORY OF ALCOHOL IN AMERICA

The use of alcohol dates back many centuries. Alcohol beverages date back to the very early part of man's history. Many archaeologists believe that wines made from grapes have existed more than ten thousand years and that drinks such as beer may date back even further. The Celts, ancient Greeks, Egyptians, and Babylonians all kept records of production and consumption of alcohol beverages.[1]

In ancient Greek and Roman civilizations, wine took a central place in the culture and religion of the people. It was regularly served at both religious and social gatherings and at holiday festivals.[2]

By the 1100s, beer was brewed regularly in Scotland, and by the 1300s, people in many countries around the world were drinking alcohol for various reasons. Some believed it was good for their health. In fact, many people believed it could be used as a medicine. Others simply enjoyed the taste and how drinking alcohol made them feel.[3]

By the fifteenth century, taverns all over Europe had become very popular. Workers gathered to enjoy beer and other alcoholic drinks.[4] In fact, beer became the daily drink of the European armies. A decree in 1632 by a British general noted that soldiers would receive two pounds of bread, one pound of meat, and four pints of beer every day.

Beer has been around for thousands of years.

Alcohol Comes to the New World

It was during the colonial days of the United States that alcohol became very popular. It had originally been brought to America from Europe. More alcohol was brought over onboard the *Mayflower* than water because the alcohol did not go bad, whereas water quickly became undrinkable.[5]

Soon the settlers began brewing their own alcohol. The drinking water throughout most of colonial America was not clean and could make a person deathly ill. Boiling the water, which is part of the process of making alcohol, helped clean the water. Some of the added ingredients that created beer and ale, such as barley and corn, gave the water flavor. These ingredients were also considered to be nutritional and healthy. Beer and ale were a major part of the diet of the colonists and nearly everyone drank. Even infants were fed beer, and it was especially recommended for nursing mothers. Farmers, laborers, merchants, lawyers, and craftsmen all drank beer on a daily basis. American troops were given alcohol as part of their daily rations. Alcohol made the colonists

According to historians, the American Indians who inhabited the United States before the settlers arrived rarely used alcohol. When they did drink alcohol, it was for religious rituals.[6]

feel good during rough winters and the difficult times they had to endure.[7]

Alcohol was even used to pay workers. In some cases, alcohol was used to buy votes. Since most of the colonists were living in poor conditions, drinking was also one of the few forms of entertainment.

As America expanded to the West, alcohol continued to become more popular. On the frontier, life was hard and short. People then called alcohol the "Good Creature of God." They believed it was a vital drink that gave people the extra strength they needed to perform hard manual labor.[8]

But problems arose from so much alcohol use in the colonies and throughout the West. Many more crimes were committed, and fights broke out frequently between men who had been drinking. There were more accidents, and often workers who had too much to drink could not do their jobs. Others just fell asleep on the job or staggered home early. Fires also resulted from the heat used to brew alcohol.

In the early 1600s, because of so much drunken behavior, Massachusetts began establishing laws to control the drinking and brewing of alcohol. Other colonies also tried to create laws to slow down or limit the use of alcohol. But for every new law that was created, several new taverns would open their doors. For the next three centuries, drinking alcohol continued to be very popular all throughout America. However, it was also the cause of many injuries, illnesses, and deaths.

Prohibition

In 1873, seventy women in the town of Hillsboro, Ohio, joined together to march from their church to the local saloons singing Christian songs and taking their concern for the harmful effects of alcohol to the streets. For weeks, they visited saloons, drug stores, and other establishments that sold alcohol, and got down on their knees and prayed. Soon, many merchants stopped selling alcohol. These activities, known as the Women's Temperance Crusades spread to twenty-three other states. It was these crusades that began the Woman's Christian Temperance Union (WCTU), an organization officially formed in 1874. Their goal was to spread the word about the harmful effects of alcohol. Within a few years they became the largest woman's group in the nation. They remained very active in the fight against alcohol right up to prohibition. Today, over 130-years later, they are still around and still fighting the evils of alcohol.[9]

In the late 1800s, an organization was formed in Ohio called the Anti-Saloon League. The organization's goal was to unite the many Americans who were against alcohol and to enforce antialcohol legislation. At the same time, a similar organization was formed in Washington, D.C. Membership in both organizations grew very quickly, and by the end of the nineteenth century, the two groups had united to form the National Anti-Saloon League. The motto of the organization was "The saloon must go." The Anti-Saloon League had definite ideas of how this was to be accomplished. They used local churches to carry their message to the people and to solicit the funds to run their attack on the nation's saloons.[10]

In the early years of the twentieth century, chapters of the Anti-Saloon League began to form in many states. By 1908, only four states did not have their own chapters.

The message was reaching the people in all of the states and by 1913, many states had passed laws making them "dry" states—states that were free of alcohol. The league now switched from changing local laws to creating one national law that would make alcohol illegal throughout the United States. This was Prohibition. In December 1913, four thousand Anti-Saloon League members marched down Pennsylvania Avenue in Washington, D.C., singing antialcohol, or temperance, songs. At the end of the march, the league members gave an Alabama congressman and a senator from Texas a copy of the proposed Eighteenth Amendment to the United States Constitution. The new amendment would enact Prohibition. The two legislators were in agreement with the views of the Anti-Saloon League and introduced the amendment to their respective legislative bodies, the United States Senate and the House of Representatives.

There was great debate in both branches of government. To increase the chances of getting the legislation passed, nearly twenty thousand league members went out and spoke at gatherings all over the United States. They urged people to write to their congressmen and senators, telling them to vote for the bill that would pass the Eighteenth Amendment.[11] The result was that many thousands of cards, letters, and telegrams poured into Washington. When the vote came up in 1914, the bill almost passed.

The league had lost the battle, but they continued to move forward. The United States was now engaged in World War I, so the league used the patriotism generated by the war to help their cause. They pointed out that the resources used to make alcohol were taking away from those needed for the soldiers and for the war effort.[12]

This time, when the bill was reintroduced, it passed, and the amendment became law in January 1920. The "dry" forces celebrated their victory all over the nation.[13]

The End of Prohibition

Prohibition was difficult to enforce. Stopping the illegal traffic of bootleg alcohol seemed impossible. The Anti-Saloon League had no powers to enforce the law, and their campaign to continue promoting the evils of drinking came to a halt. The churches that had provided them with money stopped doing so, believing that they had won the battle by getting Prohibition passed.

Few political leaders had any ideas on how to stop the illegal flow of alcohol across the borders from Canada or Mexico. Elected officials in state and local governments could not find the money to pay for the larger police departments that would be needed to track down and arrest the makers of illegal alcohol. The Treasury Department was put in charge of enforcing Prohibition. They had untrained Prohibition officers, who were often outnumbered by the criminal gangs who ran the speakeasies. Speakeasies were the bars that sold illegal alcohol.

In many rural parts of the country, there was little bootlegging, and alcohol was rarely found. But in cities such as New York, Chicago, Detroit, and New Orleans, illegal beer and whiskey were easily available at speakeasies.[14]

Then, in 1929, the Great Depression marked the beginning of the end of Prohibition. It became obvious that the making, transporting, and selling of alcoholic beverages would provide many more jobs and the sale of alcohol would provide a means of taxation that could be used to help the struggling economy. By 1933, thirteen years after the beginning of Prohibition, the Twenty-first Amendment to the Constitution repealed the Eighteenth Amendment, and Prohibition was over. With this vote, the states were now, once again, in control of liquor laws.[15]

Following the end of Prohibition, the makers of alcoholic drinks took it upon themselves to make sure that all advertisements clearly explained that drinking alcohol was only for responsible adults. Some of the first ads that appeared after Prohibition was repealed follow:

"We Who Make Whiskey Say: 'Drink Moderately'" (1934)

"Drinking and Driving Do Not Mix" (1937)

"Some Men Should Not Drink" (1938)[16]

The Later Half of the Twentieth Century

Although Prohibition was repealed in 1933, it took until 1975 for the per capita (per person) level of alcohol consumed to reach the level it was at in 1919, the year before Prohibition was enacted.[17]

MYTH		FACT
You cannot get drunk on a couple of beers or on a few glasses of wine.	vs.	While wine and beer have less alcohol content than whiskey or other so-called "hard liquors," both drinks contain alcohol, which means that you can get drunk from either.

Throughout the rest of the twentieth century, great debates continued regarding ways to make drinking safer. Some states enacted laws regarding where and when alcohol could be sold. A few states even maintained their own state prohibition. Kansas did not accept the repeal and did not allow alcohol to be sold or consumed until 1948. Oklahoma accepted the repeal in 1957 and Mississippi in 1966.[18]

By the 1950s, the National Institutes of Health was conducting more in-depth studies on alcoholism, and they began publishing their findings about the nature of the disease. They received support in their research from the makers of alcohol, including the Distilled Spirits Council of the

United States (DSCUS), a national association of alcohol producers who have worked together to combat alcohol abuse and encourage responsible drinking.[19]

In the 1950s and 1960s, drinking became more popular on college campuses. Students drank beer and behaved in a rowdy and sometimes dangerous manner. Injuries and deaths resulted from drinking at fraternity parties and other college activities.[20] As a result of such tragedies, by the end of the 1960s, the drinking age was raised from eighteen to twenty-one in every state in an effort to stop teens from drinking and hurting themselves or someone else.

In 1970, the National Institute on Alcohol Abuse and Alcoholism (NIAAA) was formed. The government organization is part of the National Institutes of Health, which has many different branches devoted to health and safety issues.

The NIAAA conducts scientific research about the health risks and benefits of drinking alcohol. They try to find treatment for alcohol-related problems, ways to prevent people from becoming alcoholics, and ways to help people who suffer from alcoholism. They work with many other national, state, and local organizations to share

Driving while intoxicated is not only dangerous, it can be deadly.

the information that they find about alcohol and alcoholism. In addition, they also work to create programs that will help prevent underage drinking.[21]

One of the most significant concerns to emerge over the past fifty years was that of drinking and driving. As more and more cars filled the roads, there were many more deaths resulting from drunk drivers. In 1980, Mothers Against Drunk Driving (MADD) was formed by a group of mothers who had lost their children in accidents resulting from drunken driving.

Over the past twenty-four years, MADD has grown, and now six hundred chapters exist all over the country. They have been instrumental in changing over twenty-three hundred state laws to include very strict penalties for anyone who drinks alcohol and drives.[22]

Many organizations, such as Alcoholics Anonymous (AA), Al-Anon, and Alateen, try to help both adults and teens who have drinking problems. They also offer help to friends and families of alcoholics.

Those Funny Beer Ads

Many of the funniest commercials seen on television are for beer. One commercial has a guy who wants to impress his date in the backseat of a limo and pops open a mini bar while accidentally sending her tiny dog high in the air. There is another one with the same guy leaning on an outhouse with his date inside. He accidentally knocks the outhouse over, and it rolls down a hill.

While the makers of beer want you to laugh, they also have a responsibility to the community. Limitations are placed on alcohol advertising, such as not showing anyone drinking the alcohol and not having minors in the commercials.

Adults should be responsible when they go out for an evening. They can have a designated driver or call a taxi.

MYTH		FACT
Most kids who drink do it instead of using illegal narcotics.	VS.	Studies show that teens who drink are 7.5 times more likely to use other illegal drugs and fifty times more likely to use cocaine than young people who never drink.[23]

Liquor manufacturers as well as local towns, cities, and even national organizations have also put together commercials. Some commercials are aimed at adults, telling them to drink responsibly, and others are designed to tell teens not to drink. Throughout the 1970s, the Distilled Spirits Council of the United States partnered with the National Football League (NFL) and the Education Commission for several years to create and broadcast national television and radio messages helping parents educate young people about alcohol. The award-winning commercials featured famous football players talking about not drinking.[24]

A recent popular commercial showed a man driving up to a party, getting out of a car, and puncturing the tires on his own car. While damaging property is not recommended, it was intended as a message to himself and to others that it is important to do whatever it takes not to drive after you have been drinking.

In the late 1990s, however, underage drinking continued to increase.[25] One major concern was that the beer commercials were so popular that they were getting kids interested in drinking. Many education, health, and family organizations have met with government officials to request that there be a ban on television alcohol commercials. Even leading sports columnists and sports figures, such as former University of Nebraska football coach and current congressman Tom Osborne, have raised concerns about too much youth exposure to alcohol advertising on sports programs.[26]

The television networks, however, make a great deal of money from sponsors such as the beer brewing companies to pay for their programs and sporting events. They could not afford to lose the money they make from such advertising.

The beer industry is particularly influential in the media, and even though they want people to be responsible drinkers, they are still in business to make money. In 1997, the head of one of the largest brewing companies in the United States told the shareholders of the company, "We are not a social service agency that happens to make beer. We are a beer company . . . and that means selling as much beer as we can."[27]

In 2001, beer and ale companies spent over $695 million to advertise their products on television.[28]

When asked to choose their favorite television commercial in a spring 2002 study, more teens named commercials for Budweiser than for any other brand, including Pepsi, Nike, and Levi's.[29]

Young people ages twelve to twenty saw more television ads for beer and ale in 2001 than for fruit juices and fruit-flavored drinks; gum; skin care products; cookies and crackers; chips, nuts, popcorn, and pretzels; sneakers; noncarbonated soft drinks; or jeans.[30]

According to a media research center, all of the top fifteen television shows aimed at least partially for teen audiences contained alcohol advertisements.[31]

CHAPTER FOUR

THE EFFECTS OF ALCOHOL ON THE BODY

It is a cool evening as paramedic Jarad Rosenberg gets the call. A thirteen-year-old boy has been reported lying along the side of a road at night. Rosenberg gets into his EMS vehicle and drives to where the boy, Nick,* was reportedly seen. He gets out of the vehicle and tries to talk to Nick,

*not his real name

Many EMS workers have to answer calls to help save lives of people who have been in accidents.

who is unable to speak, stand up, or do almost anything. He has vomit all over himself.

"Initially what we worry about the most is the management of the person's airway," explains Rosenberg. "We don't want someone to swallow and possibly choke on his or her own vomit. The nose and throat need to be clear enough so a person can breathe."[1] Rosenberg points out that, in some extreme cases, a paramedic or doctor can put a tube down the person's throat and actually breathe for him or her if necessary.

From the EMS vehicle, Rosenberg brings medication. He gives Nick a medicine that will stop the effects of a drug or narcotic. This is given in case the boy has also taken other drugs. He then gives Nick thiamine, which is vitamin B. That helps to break down the alcohol in the body. He also gives him sugar and an IV fluid, which is pumped directly into the bloodstream.

Nick is rushed to a nearby hospital emergency room. His blood alcohol level is more than 0.30 percent, which is very high and potentially deadly. In the hospital, a tube is immediately inserted into Nick's nose and goes all the way down through his throat and into his stomach to suck out the alcohol. The doctors continue to get other fluids into him so he is not dehydrated. They also want to make sure his kidneys are still functioning properly so there is no damage or infection.

Some twelve hours later, Nick leaves the hospital with his parents. Until they received a phone call from the hospital, Nick's parents never even knew he had snuck out the night before. He had apparently been to a party after his soccer game, had consumed alcohol, and had wandered away from the house where the party was taking place. "He was lucky someone saw him lying

Many teens think they can handle alcohol. They do not realize kids and teens have a low tolerance for alcohol.

there on the side of the road and called for help," says Rosenberg, who has seen many very drunk teenagers dropped off by friends near the road—sometimes not far from home and other times far away. "If they are lucky, someone calls for help."[2]

The effects of alcohol on the body will vary for different people based on their size, weight, and other factors. Someone who has not eaten in several hours may feel greater effects of alcohol than someone who has just eaten a heavy meal.

If an individual has mixed alcohol with drugs, the combination can be very dangerous, even deadly. "Kids and teens often have a low tolerance for alcohol and can get drunk more easily than an adult who weighs more and is more familiar with alcohol," adds Rosenberg.[3]

Captain John Kapica of the Greenburgh Police Department in Westchester, New York, explains that alcohol dehydrates the person to a degree, but a drug like ecstasy dehydrates an individual even more. "When the two are mixed together and that person is dancing and perspiring at a party, the body will become extremely dehydrated and cause a very high fever. In many cases the person will collapse. We've taken kids to the hospital with a 104 or 105 temperature," says Captain Kapica. "This combination could kill a person."[4]

Effects of Alcohol on the Body

When you drink alcohol, it depresses the body's central nervous system by acting like a tranquilizer, which is a medicine that makes people very relaxed. In some people, the first reaction may be stimulation, but as drinking continues, the drowsy, relaxing effects occur. As the alcohol travels throughout the bloodstream, it affects the communication between brain cells and the body. It affects areas of thought, emotion, and judgment. In sufficient amounts, alcohol can impair speech and muscle coordination, and produce sleep.[5]

How the Body Responds to Alcohol in the Bloodstream

What does it mean if a person has a 0.02 or 0.08 percent alcohol level in their bloodstream?

Although most people think alcohol will lift their spirits and make them "more fun to be around," the reality is that it is a depressant. A depressant is a substance that causes people to feel "down" or sad. The more someone drinks, the more he becomes intoxicated. The more intoxicated he gets, the less he can control what he says or does. The person may also get more anxious.

The blood alcohol concentration (BAC) is the level of alcohol that shows up in the bloodstream. A BAC level of 0.02 or 0.03 percent, means that the depressing effects of alcohol will not usually occur. Instead, people may become

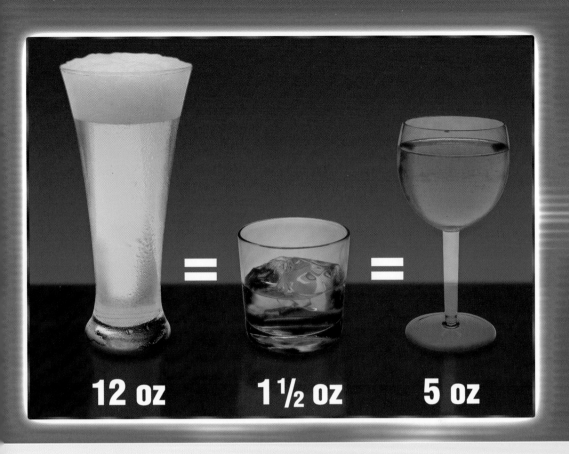

Standard servings of beer, distilled spirits, and wine each contain the same amount of alcohol.

less shy and get a feeling of great happiness. It can be hard to stop drinking once someone gets started. The more a person drinks, the less happy and more depressed he will get. This is what many people often forget. They think that by drinking more it will make them happier, but alcohol does not work that way.

By a 0.04 to 0.06 percent BAC level, a person will typically feel very relaxed. He may have

Effects of drinking for a 140-pound woman	Blood Alcohol Content
Attention may decrease	.01
Reaction time slows	.02
Tracking and steering affected	.03
Vision impaired	.04
Coordination decreases	.05
Judgment impacted	.06
	.07
Legal limit; hard to concentrate or control speed	.08
Marked loss of coordination and judgment	.09
	.10

lowered inhibitions, allowing him to do things he might otherwise be too shy to do. Most often the person does not use good judgment and makes bad decisions. This might mean hanging out with the wrong people or doing something that might be dangerous.

When the BAC level reaches 0.07 to 0.09 percent, motor skills will become more seriously impaired. It is illegal and very dangerous to drive at this level of intoxication. A person's judgment and self-control are significantly affected, and it is common to make bad decisions. Many car accidents occur because someone who has had this amount to drink can sometimes convince other people, and themselves, that he is OK to drive. The person's coordination is affected by the alcohol, and he should not be driving. It is unlikely that he will be able to react fast enough to stop at a traffic light or avoid another car making a turn.

Once the BAC reaches 0.10 percent or higher, significant impairment of motor skills and coordination will occur. A person may start slurring his speech and start losing his balance. Vision may be blurred and reaction time is much slower than usual. Even a person's hearing may be affected.

No matter how many alcoholic drinks a person has, he or she should not drive.

It is illegal to operate a motor vehicle in all states at this level of intoxication.

As the BAC exceeds 0.16 percent, the effects also include becoming restless and much more anxious. At this point, a person will often get nauseous and may start throwing up. The drinker now has the appearance of being a "sloppy drunk"—stumbling around without much control over what he says or does. There are many stories of people who have done things they regret, sometimes injuring themselves or other people and not even remembering what they did.

Should the BAC level reach a level as high as 0.25 percent, the person will usually need help walking. He will be totally confused mentally. A person at this point will frequently get very ill. At a level of 0.30 percent, most people will lose consciousness. Higher levels of alcohol can kill a person.[6]

One night of drinking is not the only way in which alcohol can affect the body. Over time, the buildup of alcohol can affect vital organs such as the liver, the heart, or even the brain. Exposing the brain to alcohol during adolescence may be damaging to the development of the brain and cause learning impairment, which means limiting the process by which someone learns. It can also cause someone to have drinking problems when he or she is older.[7]

A study conducted by researchers compared short-term memory in teens, ages fifteen and sixteen. The teens that were dependent on alcohol had a harder time remembering words and recognizing designs after just ten minutes than those who were not dependent on alcohol.[8]

Effects of Alcohol on the Adolescent Brain

Inside a person's brain, alcohol interferes with the communication between nerve cells and other cells.

Studies have shown that the younger, developing brain can be more seriously affected by the use of alcohol than older, mature brains.

In 1995, researchers at Duke University conducted experiments that showed that alcohol can have a greater effect on memory formation in younger brains than in older ones. A psychology professor who worked on the experiments explained that even moderate or occasional drinking might impair the brain's memory systems in a younger person.[9]

A key process in the memory process, known as long-term potentiation (LTP), is a means of sending memory pathways to the brain. Studies have shown that alcohol blocks the initiation of LTP in younger brains but did not have the same effect on an older brain.[10]

More recent studies done through brain imaging, called SPECT scans, show that alcohol can actually shrink the brain. In adolescents and adults

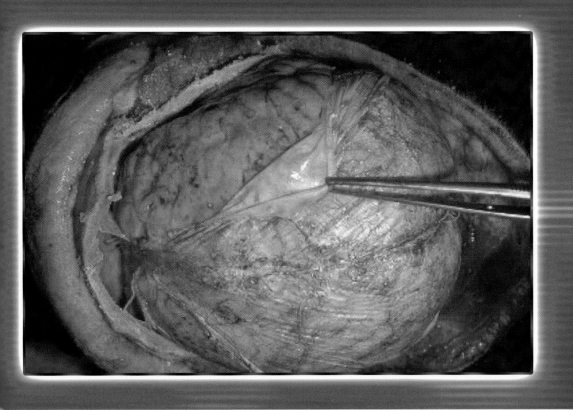

During an autopsy, this brain of an alcoholic was found to be inflamed. Drinking causes permanent brain damage.

who regularly drink large amounts of alcohol, the blood vessels in the brain constrict (or get smaller), and brain activity slows down.[11]

Alcoholics and Alcohol Abusers

There is a difference between an alcoholic and someone who abuses alcohol. An alcoholic is an individual who suffers from the disease known as alcoholism.[12] The disease begins with increased tolerance to alcohol, intense pleasure associated with drinking, and a lower sensitivity to alcohol. The disease then progresses, or grows, through stages.

"Alcohol abusers" is a recent term given to people who have long been called "problem drinkers." A problem drinker typically drinks too much in an effort to make dealing with other parts of his or her life easier. Rather than just easing the problems, however, by abusing alcohol, the person affects other aspects of his or her life. For example, the person may miss classes and fail a course, fight with family members, skip family obligations, miss days of work and even lose a job, or allow drinking to interfere with other important activities.[13]

The alcohol abuser can usually stop the cycle of drinking. This, however, means recognizing the problem and getting help, which for many alcohol abusers, is not easy.

There are an estimated 14 million people in the United States with alcohol problems who do not show signs of being in one of the stages of alcoholism. The highest percentage of people with an alcohol problem are between the ages of eighteen and twenty-nine. While some of those

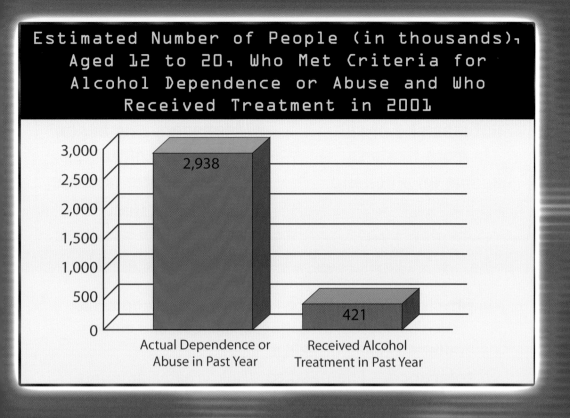

2,938

421

Actual Dependence or
Abuse in Past Year

Received Alcohol
Treatment in Past Year

individuals are of legal drinking age, obviously all those in the eighteen to twenty-one age range are not, which is why there is a strong effort to help fight underage drinking.[14]

Alcoholism

Alcoholism, also known as alcohol dependence, is a disease that includes the following four symptoms:

craving—A strong need, or urge, to drink.

loss of control—Not being able to stop drinking once drinking has begun.

physical dependence—Withdrawal symptoms, such as nausea, sweating, shakiness, and anxiety after stopping drinking.

tolerance—The need to drink greater amounts of alcohol to get "high."

According to the National Institute on Alcohol Abuse and Alcoholism, the craving that an alcoholic feels for alcohol can be as strong as the need for food or water.[16] Many alcoholics continue to drink despite serious family, health, or legal problems.

Like many other diseases, alcoholism is chronic, meaning that it lasts for a person's lifetime. Sometimes it is inherited. However, this does not mean that all children of alcoholic parents will become alcoholics. In other cases, someone with no history of alcoholism in his or her family will become an alcoholic.

The best time to stop someone from becoming an alcoholic is in what is called the prealcoholic stage—before the person becomes an alcoholic. This is when he or she starts showing signs of alcoholism. The person starts drinking more frequently and consumes more alcohol each time he or she drinks. Usually the individual is unaware that he or she finds more and more occasions for drinking.[17]

Alcoholics can receive help and treatment to better understand and deal with the disease. Many treatment centers all over the country work with alcoholics to help them understand that they are not bad people, but that they have a disease. Alcoholics Anonymous (AA) is a well-known national organization of men and women who share their experiences and provide each other with hope and strength. Members attend meetings and follow a program designed to help them stay sober.

Al-Anon, and Alateen (for younger members), is an organization that has been around for fifty years to help the family members of alcoholics try to find solutions to the problems faced by living with an alcoholic.

CHAPTER FIVE

ALCOHOL AND YOUR SOCIAL LIFE

Claire* was a freshman in high school, kind of shy, and never drank much before. At this particular party, however, she really wanted to fit in. It just so happened that she liked one of the guys, a junior named Mike, who was also invited.

That night at the party she hung out with several kids, including the guy

*not her real name

she liked. Several of the other kids were drinking, so she also grabbed a beer and started to drink. After a while, she started kissing Mike. The beer had taken away her shyness, and she was acting in a manner in which she usually did not act. But the beer did not sit well in her stomach. Suddenly she threw up on herself, him, the floor, and the couch, in front of her friends.

Humiliated as she was, her embarrassment did not end there. The next day in school, word quickly spread. Every time she walked past a group of kids, they would all make a barfing noise and start laughing. This went on for days, and after a while she could not even concentrate on her schoolwork. She just wanted to go home and crawl under the covers. It was a long time before she even considered drinking again.[1]

Wendy is a high school alcohol and drug counselor. She says unfortunately things like what happened to Claire happen all the time. "Some kids want to be cool, but they end up making real fools of themselves. Sometimes it leads to more than just embarrassment. In fact, it can really mess up someone's life."[2]

For example, Wendy tells the story of another kid who was actually drinking while he was in

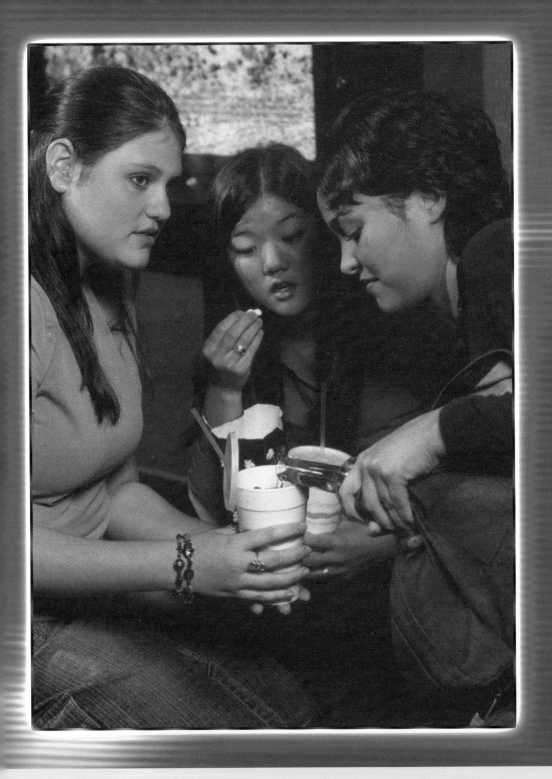

Some kids drink because they think it makes them look cool.

school. Someone caught him, and when they tried to get him to stop, he ran away. He ran out of the school and toward his car. His friends and some teachers chased him trying to stop him, but he got into the car, pulled out quickly, and started to drive. He drove right into a tree on school grounds.

Fortunately, he was not badly injured. The police arrested him in front of all of his friends and some of his teachers. His troubles did not end there. He was suspended from school for a week, and his parents took him for a drug and alcohol assessment. This meant his need to use drugs or alcohol would be analyzed, and a determination would be made as to what type of treatment he might need. It was decided that he should be sent to an alcohol rehabilitation clinic, which is where counselors work with individuals who have drinking problems to help them work on solving their problems.

Wendy is not your old-fashioned type of counselor. She does not lecture or give speeches. She likes being seen around the school and makes an effort to get to know the students.

"My door is always open," says Wendy. "I want kids to know that if they have a problem with

Smart and Realistic Ways to Stay Sober in a Not-So-Sober Situation

- Enter a party with a friend and make a pact that neither of you will drink. This way you always have someone to hang out with, and even leave with, if the party gets out of control.

- Have a great sense of humor. If people tease you for not drinking, you can simply go along with it and make some jokes about yourself being a "non-drinker." The real joke will eventually be on them when they get sick or busted and you do not.

- Take on a role or "job" at the party, such as cooking, serving food, or acting as the DJ. Get busy, so you will not have time to "hang out and drink."

- Be honest and straightforward when someone asks you if you want to drink by saying, "No thanks, I'm not into that."

alcohol or drugs that doesn't mean they are a bad kid or a druggie . . . it just means that they've got some problems like everybody else and it's okay to come in and talk about them."[3]

What happens most of the time when the kids are talking with Wendy is that they begin to see a pattern. Bad grades, embarrassing situations, trouble with the law, trouble at home, breakups with friends, or making poor choices are some of the things they find have happened much more often when they were drinking.

"Kids think the act of drinking will make them fit in, but they don't really think about how it can mess them up in so many other ways . . . and it almost always does," says Wendy.[4]

Many people, not just teens, use alcohol to help them cope in situations where they may feel anxious or nervous. People who are particularly anxious in social situations will even avoid such situations if there is no alcohol available. The problem is that the person begins to believe that he or she cannot function socially without alcohol, which is not true. However, having low self-confidence, he or she continues drinking in all social situations.[5]

Top Ten Reasons Not to Drink

1. If you accidentally kill yourself or someone else, you will not get a second chance.
2. It is too easy to lose your temper and act in a violent manner.
3. You might do something or act in a manner that you will later regret.
4. Drinking can do damage to your body.
5. Drinking can affect the memory process in your brain.
6. Getting busted and being ordered by a judge to spend time in a rehab center will take you away from your friends and family.
7. Drinking can make you feel very depressed.
8. You will smell bad.
9. The following day your head will really feel like it is going to explode. That is called a hangover.
10. You may act in ways that cause you to embarrass yourself in front of your friends, family, teachers, and/or other people that you know.

Getting Out of Control

As Captain John Kapica explains, one of the biggest problems today is binge drinking. "The problem is that kids can't drink as much as they think they can, and they end up getting very sick and even passing out," says Captain Kapica.[6] As one nineteen year old said about drinking contests, "What's the point of winning a contest if you're too sick to remember it?"[7]

A research study by the Harvard University School of Public Health showed how serious a problem binge drinking is on American college campuses. The study included questions answered by eighteen thousand students. First, binge drinking was defined as having five drinks in a row for a male, or four drinks in a row for a female, and doing this at least once or more during a two-week period. Forty-four percent of the students in the survey were considered binge drinkers. Thirty-seven percent say that they did something after binge drinking that they later regretted, and 26 percent say they forgot where they were and what they did.[8]

Peer pressure is sometimes how a person gets introduced to binge drinking. For example, sometimes in order to join a fraternity, sorority, or a club, the pledge (the person who wants to join) is asked to drink a lot to prove he or she is worthy of being a member. The idea is that it is cool to see how much alcohol a person can consume at a given time. "The problem is you can't just fill your body up with alcohol," says one seventeen-year-old female high school student. "It's going to affect your heart, your liver and other stuff."[9]

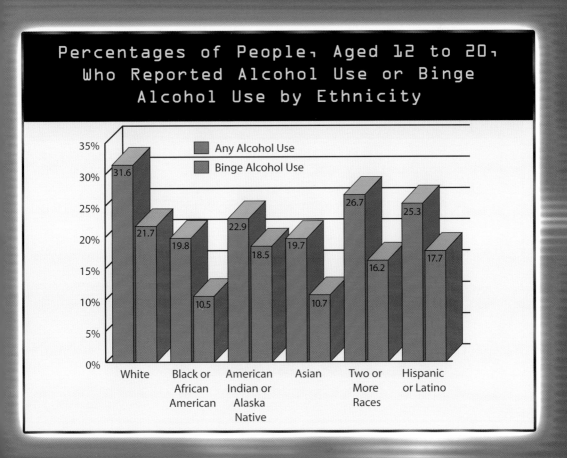

Percentages of People, Aged 12 to 20, Who Reported Alcohol Use or Binge Alcohol Use by Ethnicity

Estimated Number (in thousands) of People, Aged 12 to 20, Who Reported Alcohol Use or Binge Alcohol Use in 2001

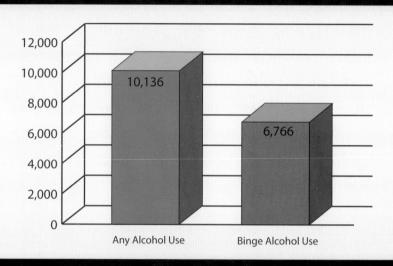

Any Alcohol Use — 10,136
Binge Alcohol Use — 6,766

Estimated Percentages of People, Aged 12 to 20, Who Reported Alcohol Use or Binge Alcohol Use in 2001 by Gender

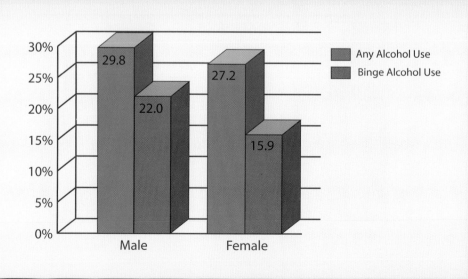

Male — Any Alcohol Use 29.8, Binge Alcohol Use 22.0
Female — Any Alcohol Use 27.2, Binge Alcohol Use 15.9

Any Alcohol Use
Binge Alcohol Use

James, an eighteen-year-old student, wanted to be part of a fraternity at Rutgers University. He drank twenty-four ounces of hard liquor, which would be like drinking two beer bottles full of whiskey (which contains a much higher percentage of alcohol than beer), in less than an hour as part of the pledging ritual. Instead of being part of the fraternity, he died.[10]

Many teens are actually very aware of the problems alcohol can cause. In 1992, two students pledged a fraternity at the Massachusetts Institute of Technology (MIT). They saw all of the drinking and felt the peer pressure to go along, so they quit. Then they wrote a fifty-page paper and sent it to the heads of the college. The paper was all about alcohol abuse and how it should be stopped. They wanted to prevent something terrible from happening to one of their friends or fellow students. Five years later, Scott K. and eleven other new fraternity recruits at MIT spent a night drinking beer and whiskey as part of the pledge ritual to join. Scott K. was found in a coma the next day. His blood alcohol level was 0.41. He died two days later.[11]

A lot of people think males are the only ones that binge on alcohol. Many females binge, too.

ALCOHOL=BUSTED!

Courtney, a freshman, had just pledged a sorority at a university in Michigan. She went out with her friends and drank a lot to celebrate with her new sorority sisters. Unfortunately, she never got to do any of the sorority activities. Later that evening, she accidentally fell out of a sixth-floor window and died.[12]

Even though it is illegal for anyone under the age of twenty-one to have or consume alcohol, many kids still find ways to get it.

Paramedic Jarad Rosenberg has seen many kids who were binge drinking. He states, "Fortunately none of the kids I've picked up along the roadside died. I guess we've been lucky in this town . . . but in many of the other communities around here kids have died or been killed in car accidents from binge drinking."[13]

It Is Too Easy to Get Alcohol

Many kids find it easy to get alcohol. Even though it is illegal to buy alcohol if you are under the age of twenty-one, many stores will illegally sell it to a minor.[14] Many police stations send undercover cops into grocery stores or liquor stores to see if the person at the counter is checking the age of the person buying alcohol. If the counter person does not check IDs, then he or she can receive a summons or even be arrested.[15]

Some kids, even as young as eleven or twelve years of age, get an older person to buy the alcohol for them, like their big brother or sister or an older friend. If the older person gets caught giving the alcohol to someone underage or that kid gets busted, the person who bought the alcohol can be in big trouble. The same goes for parents who buy alcohol and let kids drink it at a party.

Many teenagers who are in their late teens look like they are over twenty-one years old. They get alcohol by using fake ID cards. Not only is underage drinking illegal, but having a fake ID card is also illegal. In some states, just having a fake ID card is a felony.

Store owners and people letting customers into a nightclub or a bar are supposed to check ID cards carefully. Sometimes they do not check. They can also be arrested or fined for letting someone who is underage buy alcohol.

The state of North Carolina, for example, passed new fake ID laws a few years ago to stop the use of fake IDs for buying alcohol. The laws state that:

1. It is now a crime for a person under twenty-one to use a fake ID to enter a place where alcohol is sold or consumed or to get a wristband that allows them to buy alcohol. It is already a crime for someone to allow his or her license or other identification card to be used by another person as a means to purchase or possess alcohol.

It's a CRIME
to furnish
ALCOHOL
to a minor

SAVE A LIFE, TELL 'EM NO!

 MADD OJDP Business, Transportation & Housing Agency

This poster discourages adults from buying alcohol for minors.

2. It is a criminal offense to possess or manufacture fake IDs.

3. The Division of Motor Vehicles will establish an electronic system for store owners to check driver licenses and dates of birth. This electronic device can tell if the date of birth has been changed on the ID to make it look like that person is really older than he or she is.[16]

This is the law in one state, but the laws in the other forty-nine are very similar.

Many police officers, store owners, and even teens and kids are now trying hard to spread the word that it is against the law to sell alcohol to minors.

CHAPTER SIX

NEEDING AND GETTING HELP

At seventeen years of age, Dean* stood in the courtroom before the judge. The judge read his sentence. He was ordered to attend a rehabilitation program and complete it. If he did not successfully complete the program, he would be charged with the original counts of his arrest and sentenced to

*not his real name

Drinking and then driving is a very serious crime.

jail time, which would be in a juvenile hall or a lockdown facility.[1]

How did Dean end up being sentenced before a judge? It started innocently enough. Wanting to fit in with his friends, he started drinking at parties and after school. He joined a local street gang, and soon he was drinking every day—before school, during school, after school, and in the evenings. It reached the point where he could not stop. He had been a good student, but now he

MYTH		FACT
"I can handle it."	vs.	This is the most commonly used phrase of impaired drivers.[2]

no longer cared about his schoolwork. Dean no longer even bothered trying to hide his drinking from his parents. One night, he was with his friends at a party, and they were all drinking. The party spilled out onto the streets and started getting rowdy. The cops were called and he was arrested.[3]

Inside a Rehab Facility

Rehabilitation, or rehab, programs are designed to help people work through their dependence on alcohol or other drugs. Such a dependence is a physiological craving for alcohol or another drug. Recovery is a gradual process of reentering the world with the help of ongoing psychological counseling and support.

The counselors try to help the person so that he or she can do without the need to use alcohol. It takes a lot of hard work. The program includes many group meetings and counseling sessions to talk about the problem.

"It's not an easy schedule," says Scott Finkelstein, director of Daytop Village, a rehab facility in Hartsdale, New York. "During the day the kids are in school taking classes. Any problems that occur or any type of bad behavior that takes place at the rehab center is discussed at either a group meeting, a seminar, or in one-on-one counseling."[4] Students also have peer meetings with students their own age and after-school programs every day to work on their alcohol or drug problems. "They're here for more than fifty hours a week. It's pretty intense," adds Finkelstein.[5]

Dean has completed a year and a half of the program and is doing well. "He's a few months away from graduating," says Finkelstein. "He'll have his high school degree."[6] Most rehab centers do not offer an actual school degree, so kids have to go to public school and then to the rehab center after school. At this particular center, the kids attend from 8:00 A.M. to 5:00 P.M., Mondays through Fridays, and must also attend for several hours on Saturdays. The rules are strict, and the kids must take them very seriously if they want to get through the program to avoid going to jail.

Drinking and driving do not mix. Do not get into any vehicle with a person who has been drinking. Your decision not to could save your life.

If they do not take it seriously, they do not make it through the program.

Scott Finkelstein says,

There's got to be a time when the individual says "I came here because my mother wanted me here, or because the courts made me come here, but now I want to be here for myself." This means that he or she realizes that they have a serious problem. Dean was one of the rare kids that did that. After a few months there, he realized the seriousness of his problem and started working hard to get over it. Now he has gone back to being the kid he was before all the trouble started. He's a fun kid with a lot of goals ahead of him. He's going to make it.[7]

Many Do Not Make It

What happens to the kids who do not suddenly realize how important it is to get through the rehab program? Finkelstein says,

Most kids don't get through the program. Some end up in jail or juvenile hall and others die. That's just the reality. Sometimes they go back to the streets, get involved with gangs and get killed. In other cases, the drinking or mixing the drinking with drugs kills them.

They don't make it through the program for two reasons. Some don't understand that they have a real problem and are only there because someone else made them attend, usually a judge or a parent. Others don't get support outside of the treatment facility from their friends or family members, many of whom are also drinking. Very rarely do we learn that they went into another rehab program and made it through.[8]

The biggest problem faced by teens in rehab programs is functioning in the outside world where they do not receive the same level of support and are not able to open up and express themselves in the same manner as they can in the facility. Sometimes kids learn a lot about themselves and clean up their acts while in a rehab

MYTH		FACT
If you eat a lot before you drink, you will stay sober.	VS.	Food will delay the absorption of alcohol, but you will get just as drunk.[9]

Pacing Yourself

People of legal drinking age can also learn safe guidelines for drinking alcohol.

One suggestion is that when the individual is in a situation where alcohol is being served, he or she should start the evening with a tall glass of a nonalcoholic beverage. This will satisfy his or her initial thirst and the tendency to gulp the first drink down. It also postpones the introduction of alcohol into the body.

If the second drink is an alcoholic drink, he or she will drink it more slowly. He or she should then make the third drink a nonalcoholic drink. This will limit the amount of alcohol consumed and satisfy the need to drink at a social function.

This can be a suggestion for parents, friends, or anyone you know of legal drinking age who is going to a place where alcohol is served.[10]

program where they interact with counselors and other kids who have the same problems. The difficulties typically begin when they get out. They do not learn the survival skills they need to make it on the streets. Instead of trying to make new friendships or having enough inner strength to steer clear of other people who are drinking alcohol, they get lured back into hanging out with the wrong people and get back into bad habits like drinking with their friends. "It's hard to stand up to peer pressure," adds Finkelstein. "It takes a strong kid to do it."[11]

Often, a person who has gone through rehab may have a relapse. This is where the person slips back to his or her old behaviors. It is very important that the person realizes that he or she has "made a mistake" and seeks out help quickly. Sometimes it takes a good friend or a family member who really cares about that person to step in and help.

Family

If a person is having trouble and is drinking, if his or her family is helpful and supportive, the person has a much better chance of making it through rehab successfully.[12]

Many times it is a younger brother or sister who looks up to a teenager that inspires him or her to get sober and straighten out his or her life. Many kids look at their younger brother or sister and think "I don't want him (or her) to get messed up with this stuff like I did."[13]

Sometimes family members get behind someone and help him or her through a tough time, such as getting away from drinking alcohol.

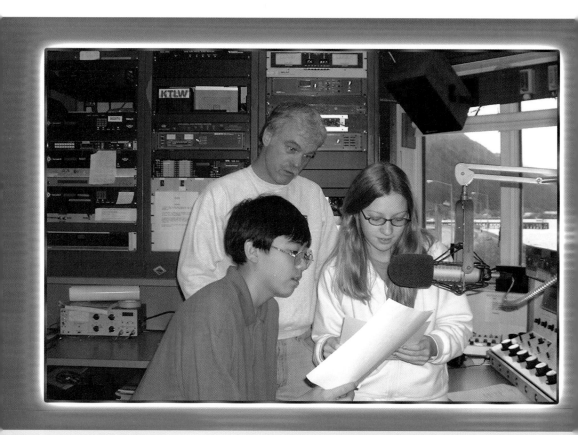

Kids can help other kids. Public service announcements on the radio help warn others about underage drinking.

Friends and peers can also help out. In fact, there are groups all over the country. Students Against Drunk Drivers (SADD) and Youth In Action (YIA) are working hard to get the message across to other kids and teens that drinking is not cool.

Unfortunately, some families are not supportive. They are in denial, meaning they do not recognize the problem. Even the person drinking may not recognize that he or she has a problem. He or she does not see himself or herself as fitting the "stereotype" or the picture that people have in their minds of what a problem drinker or an alcoholic should look and act like. "I never get drunk before noon! I can quit whenever I want! My husband and kids love me. I'm a good mother, I can't be an alcoholic," says one woman.[14] A middle-stage alcoholic reasons that because he has a major executive position in his company and earns a lot of money, he cannot be an alcoholic.[15] These people are in denial. Family members will also say similar things as a way of denying that someone has an alcohol problem or is an alcoholic.[16]

Making posters to put up in school is a good way to warn others about the dangers of underage drinking.

A Celebrity Helping Out

In the movie *Freaky Friday*, she started out fighting with her daughter but ended up being one really cool mom. But, did you know that in real life, *Freaky Friday* co-star Jamie Lee Curtis also struggled with alcohol? Today, she has turned her life around. "First and foremost I got sober to be a mother," says Curtis, who has now helped thousands of teens through a medical center teen line.[17] Over one thousand teens have been trained to work on the teen-to-teen hot line as listeners. They help each other. "The teen years are difficult," says Curtis,

> You have all this stuff flying around you—your body is changing; your relationships are changing; your hormones are changing; you're besieged by school and peer group pressures. All of that is so overwhelming for a lot of teens that they find drugs and alcohol as a temporary relief of that pressure. Eventually you realize that if you're using drugs or alcohol it's just a coping mechanism and that it's not taking care of the problem. So isn't it better to try and solve the problem than just coping with it?[18]

"The idea that alcoholics help other alcoholics is very much in sync with Teen Line," Curtis continues. "It's not adults helping teens, but teens helping teens. And that 'relatability' hopefully will allow the teen who calls up to think, 'Oh maybe you do understand me.'" Thousands of calls come in every week, letting teens open up and talk about their problems without being judged or criticized.[19]

Whether it is a hotline, such as the one Jamie Lee Curtis talks about, or talking with friends that you can trust, discussing alcohol problems is a step in treating them.

GLOSSARY

alcoholism—An excessive or compulsive use of alcoholic drinks; a disorder marked by excessive drinking of alcohol that leads to dependence or addiction.

ale—An alcoholic drink made from similar ingredients as beer, but a little bit thicker. More commonly found in the United States during colonial times.

anxious—Worried, nervous, or tense.

assessment—To review something and make a decision about it. An assessment might be done to determine how serious a problem someone has with alcohol.

decree—An order from someone with authority that has the same power as a law.

dehydrated—Suffering from a great loss of water in the body.

dependence—A very strong need for something. Someone who has a dependence on alcohol cannot stop himself or herself from the need to drink.

depressed—An inner, typically lingering feeling of sadness; a lack of any enthusiasm.

endangerment—To put someone or something in a situation that could be dangerous.

felony—A serious crime, often punishable by time in jail.

field test—A test conducted at the location outside of the laboratory or for alcohol testing, outside of the police station.

impaired—Unable to act or perform because of mental or physical restriction, which could be caused by drinking alcohol.

inhibitions—The feeling inside that holds us back from doing certain things or acting in a certain manner. To lose one's inhibitions typically means to act in a way that the person would not normally act, as is often an effect of alcohol.

intoxicated—The result of having had too much alcohol to drink, whereby it is affecting the individual's motor skills, speech, and other functions. Also known as being "drunk."

learning impairment—When the ability to learn something is being prevented because of a mental restriction that might be the result of drinking alcohol.

mandated—Ordered by someone of authority such as a judge.

mandatory—Something you must do as stated in the rules or laws.

minor—Someone under the legal age. For many things, such as voting, the legal age is eighteen. However, to drink alcohol, the legal age is twenty-one.

peer—A person who has equal standing with others in class, and/or age.

pledging ritual—Behaviors or certain acts that all newcomers to a group are asked to do in order to join (or pledge) the group. College fraternities and sororities have these rituals, called hazing. Sometimes they are simple fun activities, and other times they can be very dangerous or deadly.

Prohibition—To prohibit something. Also the term used to describe the period (1920–1933) during which the Eighteenth Amendment forbade the manufacture and sale of alcoholic beverages in the United States.

rehabilitation—To restore someone to good health or a useful life through therapy and education.

repeal—To put an end to a law by a legal act. Prohibition was repealed by the United States government in 1933.

severity—Determining how serious, or severe, something is.

sobriety—Being sober, or not having alcohol in your body.

sobriety checkpoint—A place where cars are stopped and law enforcement officers check to make sure no one is driving under the influence of alcohol.

substance abuse—Overusing or having a dependence on an addictive substance, such as alcohol or a drug.

summons—A notice telling someone he or she must appear in court.

CHAPTER NOTES

Chapter 1. Getting Caught

1. Interview with Captain John Kapica, Greenburgh Police, Greenburgh, New York, December 3, 2003.
2. Ibid.
3. Ibid.
4. Ibid.
5. Ibid.
6. Ibid.
7. Desiree Grand, Editorial Page, *The New York Journal News*, January 3, 2003, <www.thejournalnews.com/newsroom/010303/1ep03jn0103.html> (December 17, 2003).
8. Interview with Captain John Kapica, December 3, 2003.
9. Editorial Page, *The New York Journal News*, October 22, 2001, <www.thejournalnews.com/newsroom/102201/1ep01jn1022.html> (January 7, 2004).
10. Interview with Captain John Kapica, December 3, 2003.

Chapter 2. Alcohol Testing

1. Matt Holsapple, "Car Chase Leads To Purdue Student's Arrest," September 5, 2003, <www.purduenews@purdue.edu> (January 12, 2004).
2. Ibid.

3. Interview with Joe Bennett, Purdue News Service Interview, January 12, 2004.

4. Joseph S. Pete, "House Votes to Lower Legal Blood Alcohol Level," February 7, 2001, idsnews.com, <http://idsnews.com/story.php?id=3028> (December 22, 2003).

5. MedlinePlus Medical Encyclopedia, <http://www.nlm.nih.gov/medlineplus/ency/article/003632.htm> (October 15, 2004).

Chapter 3. The History of Alcohol in America

1. U.S. Department of the Treasury, Alcohol & Tobacco Tax & Trade Bureau, <http://www.ttb.gov/alcohol/history.htm> (June 16, 2004).

2. University of Pennsylvania Museum of Archaeology and Anthropology Web site, "The Origins and Ancient History of Wine," August 9, 2000, <http://www.upenn.edu/museum/Wine/wineintro.html> (November 30, 2003).

3. Gregg Smith, "Brewing in Colonial America—Part I," <http://www.beerhistory.com/library/holdings/greggsmith3.shtml> (November 25, 2003).

4. Ibid.

5. Ibid.

6. Ibid.

7. Ibid.

8. Blue Moon Web page, Steven Powell, "The Devils Drink," 2002, <http://www.bluemoon.net/~spowell/cart.htm> (January 20, 2004).

9. Woman's Christian Temperance Union Web site <www.wctu.org> (September 28, 2004).

10. Westerfield Public Library Anti-Saloon League Museum, Digital Archive, <http://www.wpl.lib.oh.us/AntiSaloon/history/> (June 15, 2004).

11. Houghton Mifflin College Web page, from Mark Moore and Dean Gerstein, "Alcohol and Public Policy: Beyond the Shadow of Prohibition" (1981) and W. J. Rorabaugh, "The Alcoholic Republic," (1979), <http://college.hmco.com/history/readerscomp/rcah/html/ah_071600_prohibitiona> (June 17, 2004).

12. Ibid.

13. Ibid.

14. Ibid.

15. Ibid.

16. Distilled Spirits Council of the United States Web page, fact sheet, <http://www.discus.org/ir/responsibility_factsheet.htm> (June 16, 2004).

17. Houghton Mifflin College Web page, from Mark Moore and Dean Gerstein, "Alcohol and Public Policy: Beyond the Shadow of Prohibition" (1981) and W. J. Rorabaugh, "The Alcoholic Republic," (1979), <http://college.hmco.com/history/readerscomp/rcah/html/ah_071600_prohibitiona> (June 17, 2004).

18. Ibid.

19. Distilled Spirits Council of the United States Web page, fact sheet, <http://www.discus.org/ir/responsibility_factsheet.htm> (June 16, 2004).

20. National Institute of Health Web page, National Institute on Alcohol Abuse and Alcoholism, <http://www.niaaa.nih.gov/about/mission.htm> (December 12, 2003).

21. Ibid.

22. Mothers Against Drunk Drivers Web site, <www.MADD.org> (June 16, 2004).

23. American Academy of Pediatrics, "Alcohol: Your Child and Drugs, Myths & Facts Page," Adapted from the AAP brochure and the AAP book, *Caring for Your Adolescent: Ages 12 to 21*, 1998 <http://www.aap.org/advocacy/chm98und.htm> (January 28, 2004).

24. Distilled Spirits Council of the United States Web site, <http://www.discus.org/ir/responsibility_factsheet.htm> (June 16, 2004).

25. Phil Mushnick, "Tasteless, Vulgar and Everywhere," *The New York Post*, Monday, September 15, 2003, p. 64.

26. Ibid.

27. Katherine Ketchum, William F. Asbury, *Beyond The Influence: Understanding and Defeating Alcoholism* (New York: Bantam Books, 2000), p. 273.

28. The Center On Alcohol Marketing & Youth Web site, fact sheet, 2003, <http://camy.org/factsheets/index.php?FactsheetID+9> (December29, 2003).

29. Ibid.

30. Ibid.

31. Reuters Web site, "Television Alcohol Ads On Rise,"

April 22, 2004, <www.reuters.com> (June 15, 2004).

Chapter 4. The Effects of Alcohol on the Body

1. Interview with Jared Rosenberg, paramedic, Greenburgh Police Department, Greenburgh, New York, January 12, 2004.

2. Ibid.

3. Ibid.

4. Interview with Captain John Kapica, Greenburgh Police Department, Greenburgh, New York, December 3, 2003.

5. E-Hospital.com, <http://www.ehospi.com/Beware/ Alcohol/HowAlcoholWorks.asp> (June 17, 2004).

6. Adapted from William J. Bailey, *Drug Use in American Society*, 3rd ed. (Minneapolis: Minn.: Burgess, 1993), <http://www.iprc.indiana.edu/ druginfo/intox.html> (December 28, 2003).

7. L. Spear, "Adolescent Brain and The College Drinker: Biological basis of propensity to use and misuse alcohol," *Journal of Studies on Alcohol (Suppl. 14)*, 2002, pp. 71–81.

8. NIAAA, "Underage Drinking: A Major Public Health Challenge," Alcohol Alert, vol. no. 59, April 2003 <http://www.niaaa.nih.gov/publications/ aa59.htm> (January 8, 2004); Study by S.F. Tapert and S.A. Brown, "Neuropsychological Correlates of Adolescent Substance Abuse: Four–year outcomes,"

Journal of the International Neuropsychological Society 5(6), 1999, pp. 481–493.

9. Duke Medical News, "Duke Medical Center Study Shows Alcohol Damages Learning More In Young Brains" December 18, 1995.

10. Ibid.

11. Katherine Ketcham and Nicholas Pace M.D., *Teens Under The Influence: the Truth About Kids, Alcohol and Other Drugs—How to Recognize the Problem and What to Do About It*, (New York: Ballantine Books, 2003).

12. Katherine Ketcham and William F. Asbury, *Beyond The Influence, Understanding and Defeating Alcoholism* (New York: Bantam Books, 2000), pp. 99–101.

13. Katherine Ketcham and William F. Asbury, pp. 99–101.

14. NIAA Treatment Information Center, Alcoholism page, <http://www.addictioncareoptions.com/alcoholism.htm> (January 20, 2004).

15. American Academy of Pediatrics, "Alcohol: Your Child and Drugs, Myths & Facts Page", Adapted from the AAP brochure and the AAP book, *Caring for your adolescent: Ages 12 to 21*. 1998 <http://www.aap.org/advocacy/chm98und.htm> (January 28, 2004).

16. Thomas Milhorn Jr., MD, Ph.D., *Drug & Alcohol Abuse, The Authoritative Guide For Parents, Teachers & Counselors* (New York: Plenum Publishing Corp., 1994), pp. 31, 33.

17. Ibid.

CHAPTER NOTES

Chapter 5. Alcohol and Your Social Life

1. Interview with Wendy Orloff, High School Drug and Alcohol Counselor, Westchester, New York, January 7, 2004.
2. Ibid.
3. Ibid.
4. Ibid.
5. Health Day News, Alcoholism: Clinical & Experimental Research, news release, "Alcohol Acts as Social Grease for the Very Nervous," December 14, 2003.
6. Interview with Captain John Kapica, Greenburgh Police Department, Greenburgh, New York, December 3, 2003.
7. Ibid.
8. Katherine Ketcham and William F. Asbury, *Beyond the Influence, Understanding and Defeating Alcoholism* (New York: Bantam Books, 2000), pp. 101–102.
9. Student interview, Fox Lane Middle School, Westchester New York, name withheld, January 27, 2004.
10. History of College Drinking Fatalities Web site, <http://www.geocities.com/CollegePark/Hall/9293/history.html> (January 18, 2004).
11. Henry Wechsler, Ph.D. and Bernice Wuethrich, *Dying To Drink, Confronting Binge Drinking And Alcohol On Campuses* (New York: St. Martin's Press, 2002), pp. 41–42.

12. History of College Drinking Fatalities Web site, <http://www.geocities.com/CollegePark/Hall/9293/history.html> (January 18, 2004).

13. Interview with Jarad Rosenberg, paramedic, Greenburgh Police Department, Greenburgh, New York, January 12, 2004.

14. Interview with Captain John Kapica, December 3, 2003.

15. Ibid.

16. North Carolina News 2 Web page, "New Fake ID Law, Possessing/Manufacturing Fraudulent Identification to Obtain Liquor," November 2001, <http://www.initiative.org/news2.shtml> (January 24, 2004).

Chapter 6. Needing and Getting Help

1. Interview with Scott Finkelstein, director, Daytop Village, Hartsdale, New York, January 19, 2004.

2. Vanderbilt University web site, Larry Axmaker, EdD, PhD, "Dispelling Myths About Drinking," Health Plus Vanderbilt University Wellness Program, <http://vanderbiltowc.wellsource.com/dh/content.asp?ID=476> (June 17, 2004).

3. Interview with Scott Finkelstein, January 19, 2004.

4. Ibid.

5. Ibid.

6. Ibid.

7. Ibid.

8. Ibid.

9. Vanderbilt University web site, Larry Axmaker, EdD, PhD, "Dispelling Myths About Drinking," Health Plus Vanderbilt University Wellness Program, <http://vanderbiltowc.wellsource.com/dh/content.asp?ID=476> (June 17, 2004).

10. Nicholas A. Pace, M.D. and Wilbur Cross, *Guidelines To Safe Drinking* (New York: McGraw, Hill, 1984), p. 119.

11. Interview with Scott Finkelstein, January 19, 2004.

12. Ibid.

13. Ibid.

14. Katherine Ketcham and William F. Asbury, *Beyond The Influence, Understanding and Defeating Alcoholism* (New York: Bantam Books, 2000).

15. Ibid

16. Ibid.

17. John Morgan with medical adviser Stephen A. Shoop, M.D., "Jamie Lee Curtis Helps Teens Cope," Spotlight Health Page, May 16, 2003, <http://www.drdonnica.com/celebrities/00006364.htm> (January 20, 2004).

18. Ibid.

19. Ibid.

FURTHER READING

Aronson, Virginia. *How to Say No*. Philadelphia: Chelsea House, 2000.

Bellenir, Karen, ed. *Drug Information for Teens: Health Tips About the Physical and Mental Effects of Substance Abuse*. Detroit: Omnigraphics, 2002.

Graves, Bonnie. *Alcohol Use and Abuse*. Mankato, Minn.: LifeMatters, 2000.

Hyde, Margaret O., and John F. Setaro. *Alcohol 101: An Overview for Teens*. Brookfield, Conn.: Twenty-First Century Books, 1999.

Johnson, Julie. *Why Do People Drink Alcohol?* Austin, Tex.: Raintree Steck-Vaughn, 2001.

Lamb, Kirsten. *Alcohol*. Austin, Tex.: Raintree Steck-Vaughn, 2002.

Lieurance, Suzanne. *The Prohibition Era in American History*. Berkeley Heights, N.J.: Enslow Publishers, Inc., 2003.

Stewart, Gail. *Teen Alcoholics*. San Diego: Lucent Books, 2000.

Internet Addresses

Alcohol & Drug Information: For Kids Only
  <http://www.health.org/features/kidsarea>
  Learn about drugs, alcohol, and more, from this site.

A Guide for Teens
  <http://www.health.org/govpubs/phd688/>
  This online brochure can help you help someone else. There is also a list of resources listed at the end.

Al-Anon/Alateen
  <http://www.al-anon.alateen.org>
  If you or someone you know has a drinking problem, check out this site.

National Association for Children of
  Alcoholics: Just 4 Kids
  <http://www.nacoa.org/kidspage.htm>
  Learn more about alcoholism, how to help, and how to cope.

INDEX

A

Al-Anon, 34, 55
Alateen, 34, 55
alcohol counselor, 11
Alcoholics Anonymous
  (AA), 34, 55
alcoholism, 53–55
    craving, 53
    loss of control, 53
    physical dependence, 54
    tolerance, 54
alcohol saliva test, 19
alcohol testing, 16
antialcohol legislation, 26
Anti-Saloon League, 26–28
arrest, 14, 15, 73

B

Babylonians, 21
blood alcohol
  concentration (BAC),
  44–49
bootlegging, 28–29
breath alcohol detector,
  17, 19
Breathalyzer™, 19

C

Celts, 20
central nervous system, 43
colonial days, 23–25

commercials, 34–38
community service, 11, 18
court, 11, 73
Curtis, Jamie Lee, 85–86
custody, 11

D

Daytop Village, 76
depressant, 43–44
Distilled Spirits Council of
  the United States
  (DSCUS), 31–32
Driving Under the
  Influence (DUI), 18
Driving While Intoxicated
  (DWI), 14, 18, 33
"dry" states, 27, 28
Duke University, 49

E

early laws, 25
Education Commission, 36
Egyptians, 21
eighteenth amendment,
  27–28
Emergency Medical
  Service (EMS), 39, 40, 41

F

field test, 16
fine, 11, 18
full pursuit, 13

INDEX

G

Great Depression, 29
Greeks, 21

H

Harvard University School
  of Public Health, 64
House of Representatives,
  27

I

illegal drugs, 8

J

jail, 74, 76
juvenile hall, 74

K

K9 unit, 13

L

law against fake
  identification, 70, 72
license suspension, 18
lockdown facility, 74
long-term potentiation
  (LTP), 50

M

marijuana, 6, 8
Mayflower, 23
Mothers Against Drunk
  Driving (MADD), 17, 33

N

National Anti-Saloon
  League, 26–28
National Football League
  (NFL), 36
National Institute on
  Alcohol Abuse and
  Alcoholism (NIAAA), 32,
  54
National Institutes of
  Health, 31

O

Osborne, Tom, 37

P

peer meetings, 76
pre-alcoholic, 55
Prohibition, 25–30
public service
  announcements, 82
Purdue University, 12, 15

R

rehabilitation program, 73,
  75–76, 78–79, 80
Rutgers University, 67

S

Scotland, 21
sobriety checkpoint, 12,
  15, 16
sobriety test, 16
speakeasy, 29

Students Against Drunk Drivers (SADD), 83
summons, 8, 11

T

Teen Line, 85
twenty-first amendment, 30

U

underage drinking, 9, 10, 11
  child endangerment, 9
  consumption of alcohol by a minor, 15
  contributing to the delinquency of a minor, 8
  criminal confinement, 15
  criminal recklessness with a vehicle, 15
  Driving Under the Influence (DUI), 18
  Driving While Intoxicated (DWI), 14, 18, 33
  operating a vehicle under the age of 21 with a alcohol content of 0.02 percent or higher, 15
  possession of alcohol, 9
  resisting law enforcement, 15
University of Nebraska, 37
U.S. Senate, 27

W

Women's Christian Temperance Union (WCTU), 26
World War I, 28

Y

Youth In Action (YIA), 83